Inhalt

1 What belongs in the schoolbag?

Help Sherlock and circle all school things.

2 Look at the picture and answer the questions.

How many = Wie viele

How many schoolbags can you see? ________

How many red pencils can you find? ________

How many books are on the desks? ________

How many pupils are working with scissors? ________

3 Colour the frame.

4 Listen and draw lines.

Key: 449

rubbers	20
pen	2
pencils	8
books	1
rulers	1
pencil case	3

5 Fill in.

1. Buch
2. Radiergummi
3. Klebstoff
4. Lineal
5. Füllfeder

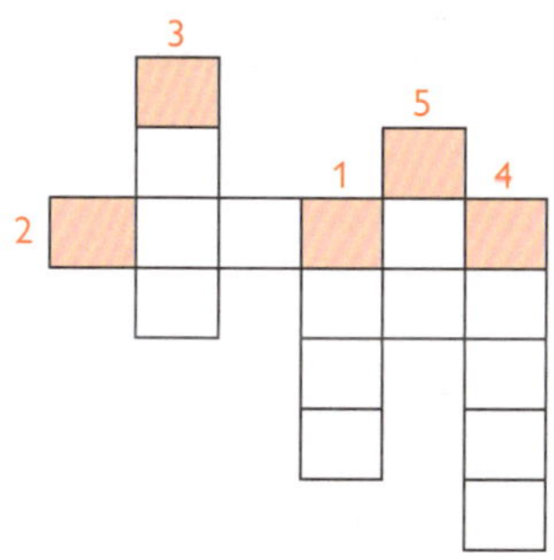

1 Help Sherlock to find the match and draw lines.

grey white orange yellow green pink

black red blue brown

2 Write the numbers in the correct order.

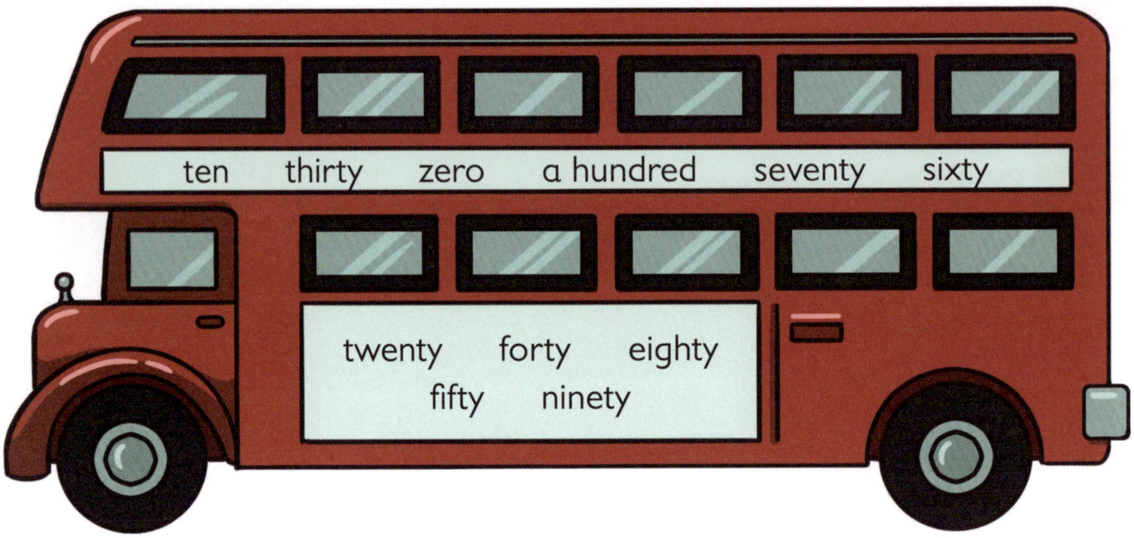

zero, ______________________________

____

3 What colour is the number?

twenty nine fifty zero
eighty seventy five thirty

0 = ________ 9 = ________ 30 = ________ 70 = ________

5 = ________ 20 = ________ 50 = ________ 80 = ________

4 How many?

Read the sentences and listen to the audiofile. Draw a ☺ or a ☹.

Key: 510

Sherlock has got sixty £ in his pocket. ☐

There are seven birds in the cage. ☐

A hundred little ladybirds are flying in the sky. ☐

The British Guard is talking to two tourists. ☐

My brother is twenty years old. ☐

5 Listen and talk. (Sprich den Text mit.)

Key: 564

A hundred black-white magpies
are coming after you.
They want to steal your necklace –
don't let this happen to you!

Wave your hands and shout out loud:
"Hey you, you shouldn't steal my things
by flapping your wings.
I don't want you to stay!"

<u>So ten scared magpies quickly fly away!</u>

Ninety black-white magpies
are coming after you.
They want to steal your necklace –
don't let this happen to you!
...

1 Can you help Sherlock Holmes to find the words?

ear eye hair head knee mouth nose shoulder toe

T	H	D	N	I	Z	W	D	Z	Y	U	P	T	J	E	J	U	H	Q	Q
G	M	U	L	N	A	J	F	S	Y	K	T	H	B	P	V	E	C	T	Y
S	E	P	K	J	I	C	J	G	L	N	U	E	N	E	P	U	V	D	I
B	T	J	W	A	O	C	J	Q	Q	J	P	C	S	M	O	U	T	H	T
O	F	U	P	A	C	T	H	R	E	O	U	K	K	V	N	V	P	G	L
X	I	P	H	C	R	U	G	S	O	K	V	C	E	D	U	U	S	Y	N
H	E	Y	T	N	K	T	V	F	R	F	T	U	I	P	Y	T	D	C	X
P	S	L	Y	O	N	B	F	Q	V	H	E	N	W	Y	S	B	H	W	G
B	H	P	W	S	Y	V	N	O	T	G	J	A	G	L	X	F	A	N	E
F	D	N	K	E	E	N	W	S	E	E	N	K	R	Z	X	G	I	D	Z
T	Q	L	Z	K	Y	C	R	J	H	W	X	Q	S	Q	J	D	R	Y	B
F	Q	G	T	K	G	Z	C	B	L	O	G	X	V	B	C	O	K	Q	L
P	P	X	R	A	A	N	J	P	T	D	U	D	Q	V	Q	Y	P	X	P
N	R	P	E	B	P	Q	A	C	Y	K	P	L	X	I	Z	Q	S	I	A
Z	Q	Z	C	O	K	I	M	R	T	M	Q	L	D	T	M	Q	E	S	Q
C	F	X	P	Z	N	J	D	Z	Y	W	J	Z	B	E	M	X	O	O	C
K	Q	I	J	H	A	D	G	X	O	W	G	P	L	F	R	F	T	S	O
A	Y	M	O	I	D	S	O	J	I	Q	P	E	I	S	D	A	E	H	S
Y	P	B	E	I	L	X	V	A	S	J	W	T	I	N	U	I	V	M	P
E	Y	E	C	F	E	E	R	Z	X	C	N	L	N	P	M	K	L	R	X

2 Do the crossword below.

3 Sherlock has to find out, who is saying what.

Can you help him?

☐ I have three eyes and six ears.

☐ Look at my twelve fingers and eight toes!

☐ My head looks like an apple and I have long black hair.

☐ I have a very long nose and a wide mouth.

4 Describe the alien.

The alien has three ________. ()

The alien ______________________. ()

The ______________________. ()

______________________________. ()

______________________________. ()

1 Fill in the right number.

① snake
② dog
③ budgie
④ pony
⑤ cat
⑥ fish
⑦ mouse
⑧ spider
⑨ guinea pig
⑩ hamster

2 Can pets speak as well?

Super

woof
woof

glub
glub

squeak
squeak

tweet
tweet

meow
meow

gut gemacht

3 Which pets can you spot?

body: ______ eyes: ______ nose: ______

head: ______ ears: rabbit legs: ______

4 Answer the questions:

Have you got a pet? ______ (Yes, I have. / No, I haven't.)

What is it? ______ (It is a ______.)

What is its name? ______ (Its name is ______.)

What colour is it? ______ (It's brown/white/black …)

How old is it? ______ (It is ______ years old.)

Clothes

1 What is it?

Tick the right answer!

☐ skirt ☐ cap ☐ jeans ☐ coat ☐ shoe ☐ sock

☐ sweater ☐ hat ☐ trousers ☐ shorts ☐ dress ☐ boots

☐ scarf ☐ t-shirt ☐ gloves ☐ raincoat

2 Whoops, what a mix-up!

Can you help Sherlock? Write down, which clothes you can spot.

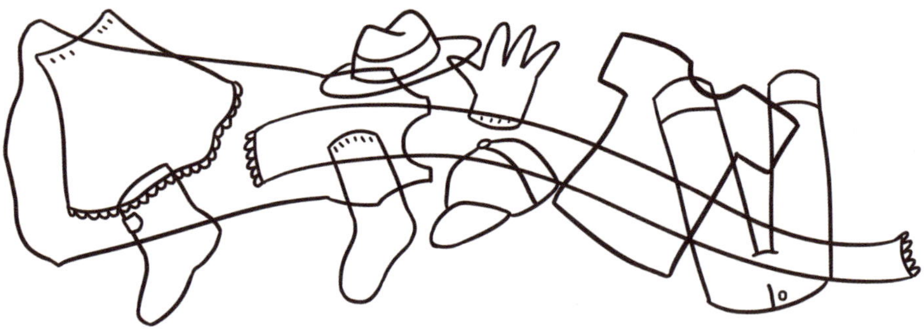

____

____

3 Window shopping!

Read the sentences and colour the clothes.

Colour the skirt yellow and the raincoat orange.
The boots for £90 are black and the hat is brown.
Colour the £30 jeans grey and the £30 boots red.
The dress for £20 is pink and the scarf is blue.
Colour the shoes for £20 grey and the gloves white.

1 Song: I have a pet

Sing along and answer the questions:

Key: 571

Which animal isn't really a pet? ______________________

Which pets does the boy have? ______________________

What colour is the dog in the video? ______________________

Which is the 3rd pet? ______________________

How often does the fish say *glub*? ______________________

2 Find the matching rhyme.

e.g. mouse – house

Numbers:	**Colours:**	**Clothes:**
pen – ________	Jack – ________	rock – ________
shoe – ________	sink – ________	blue – ________
hero – ________	Queen – ________	shirt – ________
great – ________	fellow – ________	boat – ________

3 Help Sherlock to solve the body parts Cryptogram!

A	B	C	D	E	F	G	H	I	J	K	L	M	N	O	P	Q	R	S	T	U	V	W	X	Y	Z
5							2																	9	

23	26	11	11

	H						
16	2	25	14	13	17	11	7

3	25	11

15	20	26	18	11	7

H	A		
2	5	20	7

H		A	
2	11	5	17

	A	
11	5	7

	Y	
11	9	11

26	25	16	11

				H
10	25	14	3	2

4 Do the "school things" Sudoku!

1 Help the market saleswoman to sort the fruits and vegetables.

______________________ ______________________

______________________ ______________________

carrots	apples	plums
bananas	tomatoes	pears
oranges	peppers	potatoes
onions	cucumbers	grapes

2 Do the crossword!

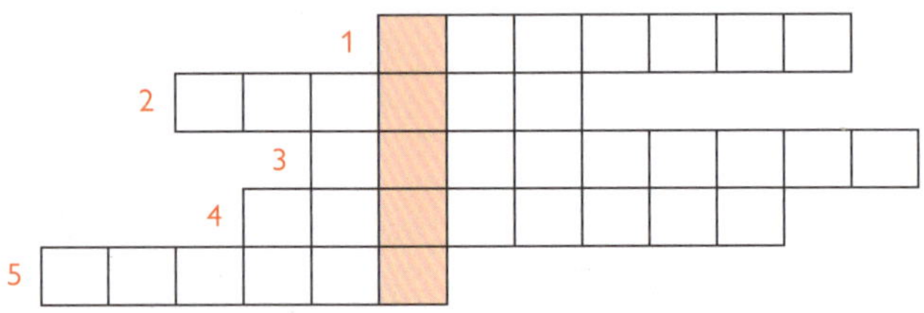

The British Guard likes __________ the most.

3 Find the match and use the same colour!

ap	ion	cucum	ange
bana	ple	or	ar
on	um	pep	rot
pl	toe	pe	ber
pota	na	car	per

Bye-bye, Sherlock!

Here you are.
That's £ 6.75.

I would like 3 apples, a kilo of strawberries and 5 red peppers, please!

Good morning, Sherlock!
How can I help you today?

Good Morning!

Thank you very much.
Good-bye!

4 Sherlock goes shopping at the market.

Complete the dialogue! What do they say?

1 How are Sherlock and the Guard feeling?

tired hungry sad happy fine angry

Tim is ________. (das)

Lucy is ________. (pahpy)

Matt is screaming.
He is ________. (nagyr)

Marc is eating. He was ________. (yuhgrn)

Ellie is asleep. She was very ________. (tired)

Dan is seeing a ghost.
He is ________. (deracs)

2 Read the questions and circle the right picture.

Who is sad?

Who is sleepy?

Who is scared?

Who is happy?

Susan is...

Oliver is...

Monica is...

Jasper is...

Jasper is angry.

1 Do you know the word?

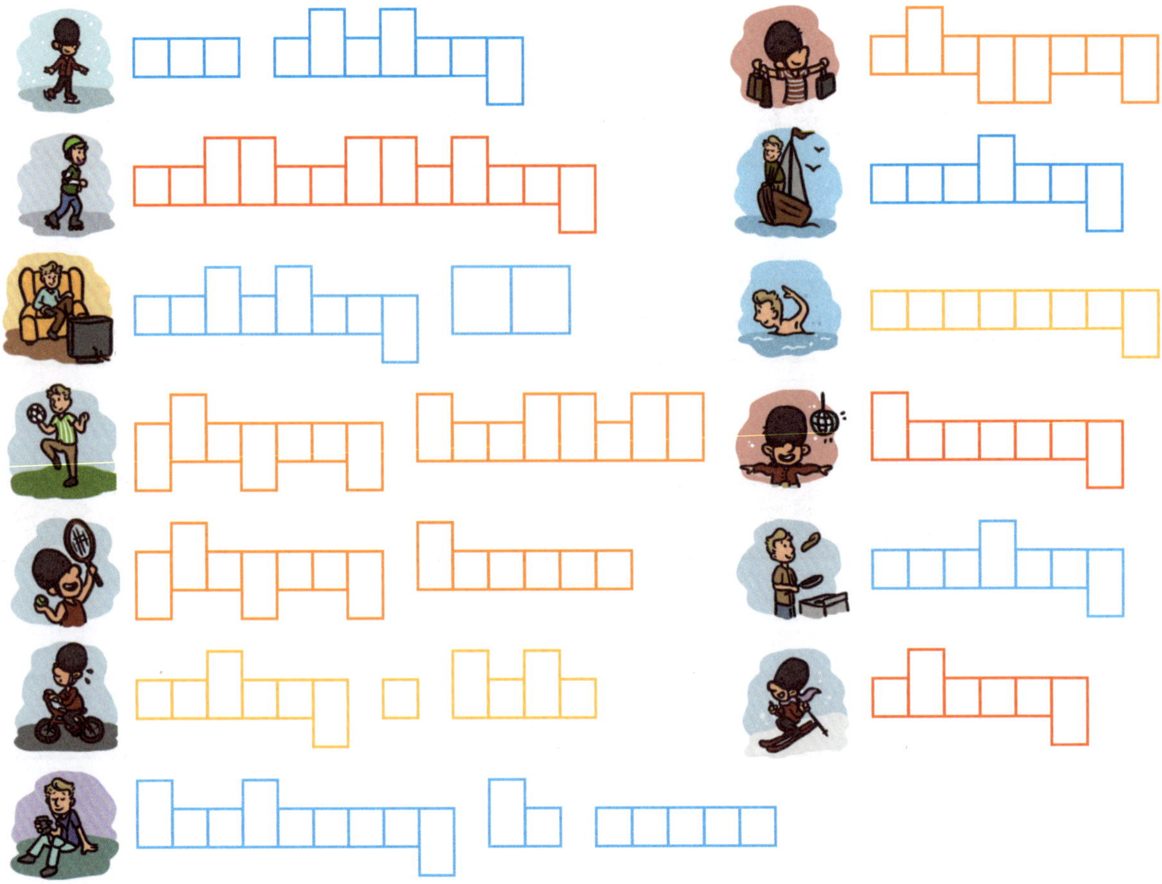

skiing	cooking	playing football	swimming	playing tennis
watching TV	ice skating	rollerblading	riding a bike	shopping
sailing	dancing	listening to music		

2 True or false?

	true ✓	false ✗
You can go ice skating in summer.	☐	☐
You need a ball if you want to play football.	☐	☐
You need money (€/£) if you want to go shopping.	☐	☐
You can cook in a swimming pool.	☐	☐
You need a book if you want to watch TV.	☐	☐

LÖSUNGEN

3

VERITAS
Gemeinsam besser lernen

Zum Heraustrennen dieses Lösungsheftes die mittlere Klammer lösen.

Liebe Eltern!

Mit diesem Ferienheft kann Ihr Kind die wichtigsten Inhalte des vergangenen Schuljahres während der Ferien wiederholen und festigen. Damit steigt es **bestens vorbereitet in die nächste Klasse** ein – ein klarer Vorteil für die weitere Schullaufbahn!
Die Inhalte werden dabei abwechslungsreich gemischt, mit spielerischen Elementen gewürzt und in 15 gut verdaulichen Tagesportionen angeboten, die die Kinder weitgehend selbstständig bewältigen können.

So können Sie Ihr Kind dabei unterstützen:

- Legen Sie gemeinsam drei Lernwochen oder 15 Lerntage fest und achten Sie auf die Einhaltung. Manchmal kann es auch hilfreich sein, eine Seite gemeinsam anzugehen!
- Mit den **herausnehmbaren Lösungen** können Sie die Ergebnisse eines Lerntages rasch kontrollieren oder das Kind selber überprüfen lassen.
- **Alle Lösungen** sind **in hellblauer Lösungsschrift** eingetragen, zeichnerische Lösungen eingezeichnet. Bisweilen gibt es neben der angegebenen Lösung noch weitere, individuell verschiedene.
- Zu guter Letzt: Die Reise durch die Aufgaben und Funpages soll für Ihr Kind ein Vergnügen sein und Spaß machen! Dann ist der Lernerfolg am größten.

Wenn Ihr Kind dieses Symbol sieht, heißt das, dass es ein Lied hören und mitsingen oder eine Übung mit einem Hörtext machen kann.
Wenn Sie einen PC zur Verfügung haben, finden Sie die Lieder und Hörtexte auf: http://ferienheft-englisch3vs.veritas.at
Wenn Ihr Kind die Lieder und Hörtexte auf seinem/Ihrem Handy anhören möchte, können Sie den Code neben der Übung mithilfe eines QR-Code Scanners (als Gratisapp verfügbar) einscannen.

Key: 123

Einen schönen Sommer wünscht Ihnen
Doris Horvath

1 What belongs in the schoolbag?

Help Sherlock and circle all school things.

2 Look at the picture and answer the questions.

How many = Wie viele

How many schoolbags can you see? *three*

How many red pencils can you find? *nine*

How many books are on the desks? *four*

How many pupils are working with scissors? *two*

3 Colour the frame.

4 Listen and draw lines.

Key: 449

rubbers	20
pen	2
pencils	8
books	1
rulers	1
pencil case	3

5 Fill in.

1. Buch
2. Radiergummi
3. Klebstoff
4. Lineal
5. Füllfeder

	3		1	5	4
	g				
	l			p	
2 r	u	b	b	e	r
	e		o	n	u
			o		l
			k		e
					r

1 Help Sherlock to find the match and draw lines.

2 Write the numbers in the correct order.

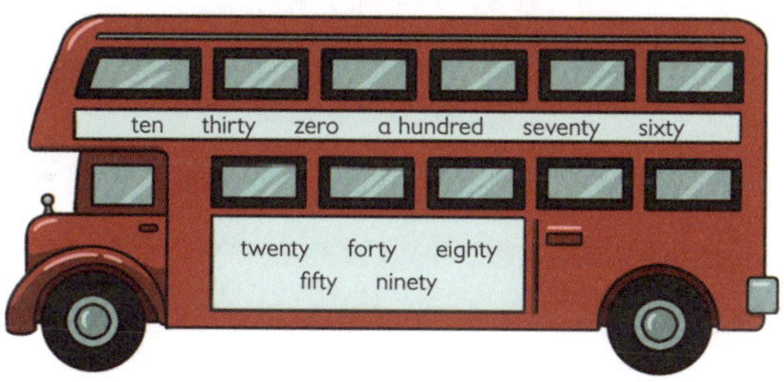

zero, ten, twenty, thirty, forty, fifty, sixty, seventy, eighty, ninety, a hundred

3 What colour is the number?

twenty nine fifty zero
eighty seventy five thirty

0 = *green* 9 = *black* 30 = *orange* 70 = *brown*

5 = *pink* 20 = *red* 50 = *yellow* 80 = *blue*

4 How many?

Read the sentences and listen to the audiofile. Draw a ☺ or a ☹.

Key: 510

Sherlock has got sixty £ in his pocket. ☺

There are seven birds in the cage. ☹

A hundred little ladybirds are flying in the sky. ☺

The British Guard is talking to two tourists. ☺

My brother is twenty years old. ☹

5 Listen and talk. (Sprich den Text mit.)

Key: 564

A hundred black-white magpies
are coming after you.
They want to steal your necklace –
don't let this happen to you!

Wave your hands and shout out loud:
"Hey you, you shouldn't steal my things
by flapping your wings.
I don't want you to stay!"

So ten scared magpies quickly fly away!

Ninety black-white magpies
are coming after you.
They want to steal your necklace –
don't let this happen to you!
...

1 Can you help Sherlock Holmes to find the words?

ear eye hair head knee mouth nose shoulder toe

```
T H D N I Z W D Z Y U P T J E J U H Q Q
G M U L N A J F S Y K T H B P V E C T Y
S E P K J I C J G L N U E N E P U V D I
B T J W A O C J Q Q J P C S M O U T H T
O F U P A C T H R E O U K K V N V P G L
X I P H C R U G S O K V C E D U U S Y N
H E Y T N K T V F R F T U I P Y T D C X
P S L Y O N B F Q V H E N W Y S B H W G
B H P W S Y V N O T G I A G L X F A N E
F D N K E E N W S E E N K R Z X G I D Z
T Q L Z K Y C R J H W X Q S Q J D R Y B
F Q G T K G Z C B L O G X V B C O K Q L
P P X R A A N J P T D U D Q V Q Y P X P
N R P E B P Q A C Y K P L X I Z Q S I A
Z Q Z C O K I M R T M Q L D T M Q E S Q
C F X P Z N J D Z Y W J Z B E M X O O C
K Q I J H A D G X O W G P L F R F T S O
A Y M O I D S O J I Q P E I S D A E H S
Y P B E I L X V A S J W T I N U I V M P
E Y E C F E E R Z X C N L N P M K L R X
```

2 Do the crossword below.

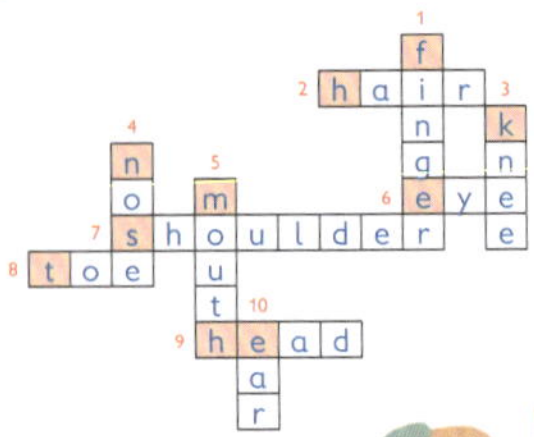

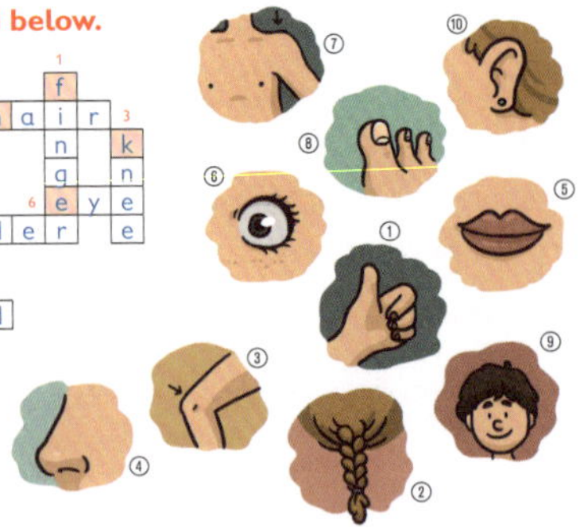

3 Sherlock has to find out, who is saying what.

Can you help him?

4 Describe the alien.

The alien has three *eyes*. ( )

The alien *has four ears*. ( )

The *alien has two arms*. ( )

The alien has six fingers. ( )

The alien has eight toes. ( )

1 Fill in the right number.

① snake
② dog
③ budgie
④ pony
⑤ cat
⑥ fish
⑦ mouse
⑧ spider
⑨ guinea pig
⑩ hamster

2 Can pets speak as well?

woof woof
glub glub
squeak squeak
tweet tweet
meow meow

3 Which pets can you spot?

body: *cat* eyes: *snake* nose: *budgie*

head: *pony* ears: *rabbit* legs: *spider*

4 Answer the questions:

Hier ist alles richtig, was du schreibst!

Have you got a pet? ______ (Yes, I have. / No, I haven't.)

What is it? ______ (It is a ______.)

What is its name? ______ (Its name is ______.)

What colour is it? ______ (It's brown/white/black …)

How old is it? ______ (It is ______ years old.)

1 What is it?

Tick the right answer!

- [ ] skirt [x] cap
- [ ] jeans [x] coat
- [x] shoe [ ] sock

- [x] sweater [ ] hat
- [ ] trousers [x] shorts
- [x] dress [ ] boots

- [x] scarf [ ] t-shirt
- [ ] gloves [x] raincoat

2 Whoops, what a mix-up!

Can you help Sherlock? Write down, which clothes you can spot.

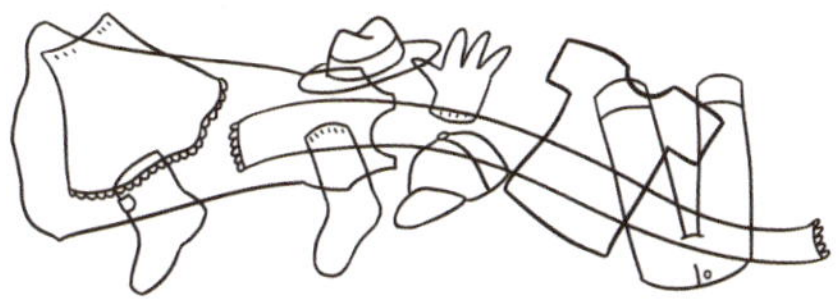

t-shirt, boot, dress, cap, scarf, skirt, sock,
hat, trousers, glove

3 Window shopping!

Read the sentences and colour the clothes.

Colour the skirt yellow and the raincoat orange.
The boots for £90 are black and the hat is brown.
Colour the £30 jeans grey and the £30 boots red.
The dress for £20 is pink and the scarf is blue.
Colour the shoes for £20 grey and the gloves white.

1 Song: I have a pet

Sing along and answer the questions:

Key: 571

Which animal isn't really a pet? lion
Which pets does the boy have? mouse, dog, bird, lion
What colour is the dog in the video? brown
Which is the 3rd pet? mouse
How often does the fish say *glub*? 7 times

2 Find the matching rhyme.

e.g. mouse – house

Numbers:
pen – ten
shoe – two
hero – zero
great – eight

Colours:
Jack – black
sink – pink
Queen – green
fellow – yellow

Clothes:
rock – sock
blue – shoe
shirt – skirt
boat – coat

3 Help Sherlock to solve the body parts Cryptogram!

A	B	C	D	E	F	G	H	I	J	K	L	M	N	O	P	Q	R	S	T	U	V	W	X	Y	Z
5			17	11	15	18	2	20		23	13	10	26	25			7	16	3	14				9	

KNEE (23 26 11 11)
SHOULDER (16 2 25 14 13 17 11 7)
TOE (3 25 11)
FINGER (15 20 26 18 11 7)
HAIR (2 5 20 7)
HEAD (2 11 5 17)
EAR (11 5 7)
EYE (11 9 11)
NOSE (26 25 16 11)
MOUTH (10 25 14 3 2)

4 Do the "school things" Sudoku!

1 Help the market saleswoman to sort the fruits and vegetables.

bananas, oranges, apples | carrots, onions, tomatoes
plums, pears, grapes | peppers, cucumbers, potatoes

carrots	apples	plums
bananas	tomatoes	pears
oranges	peppers	potatoes
onions	cucumbers	grapes

2 Do the crossword!

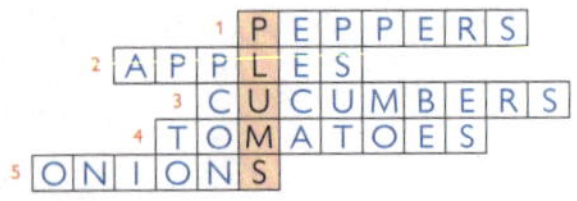

The British Guard likes plums the most.

3 Find the match and use the same colour!

ap	ion	cucum	ange
bana	ple	or	ar
on	um	pep	rot
pl	toe	pe	ber
pota	na	car	per

4 Sherlock goes shopping at the market.

Complete the dialogue! What do they say?

1 How are Sherlock and the Guard feeling?

tired hungry sad happy fine angry

Tim is sad. (das)
Lucy is happy. (pahpy)
Matt is screaming.
He is angry. (nagyr)

Marc is eating. He was hungry. (yuhgrn)
Ellie is asleep. She was very tired. (tired)
Dan is seeing a ghost.
He is scared. (deracs)

2 Read the questions and circle the right picture.

Who is sad?

Who is sleepy?

Who is scared?

Who is happy?

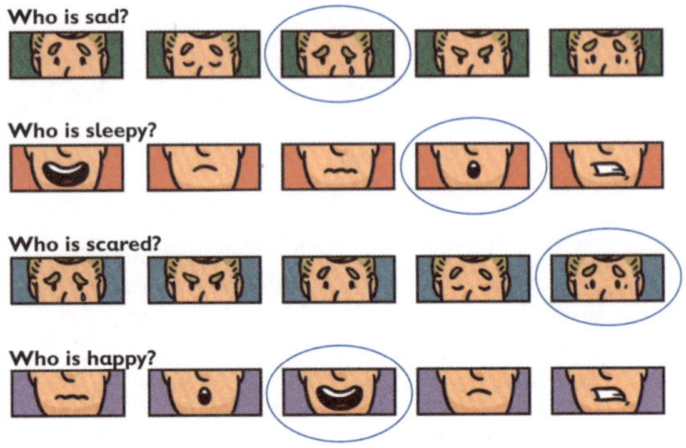

Jasper is angry.

Monica is sad.

Oliver is happy.

Susan is sleepy.

1 Do you know the word?

ice skating
rollerblading
watching TV
playing football
playing tennis
riding a bike
listening to music
shopping
sailing
swimming
dancing
cooking
skiing

skiing	cooking	playing football	swimming	playing tennis
watching TV	ice skating	rollerblading	riding a bike	shopping
sailing	dancing	listening to music		

2 True or false?

	true ✓	false ✗
You can go ice skating in summer.	☐	☒
You need a ball if you want to play football.	☒	☐
You need money (€/£) if you want to go shopping.	☒	☐
You can cook in a swimming pool.	☐	☒
You need a book if you want to watch TV.	☐	☒

3 Listen and tick the right answer.

Write a sentence!

Key: 635

Lucy	
swim	☒
go shopping	☐

Tim	
skate	☒
read books	☐

Matt	
play football	☐
play tennis	☒

Emily	
sing	☐
dance	☒

Lucy likes to *swim*.
Tim likes to *skate*.
Matt likes to play tennis.
Emily likes to dance.

Hier ist alles richtig, was du schreibst!

I like ____________, but I don't like ____________.

1 Time, time, time

I have to go to bed at *ten o'clock*.

I have breakfast at *quarter past seven*.

School finishes at *quarter to twelve*.

I want to go for a walk at *half past six*.

I get up at ________ o'clock.
I have breakfast at ____________.
I leave for school at ____________.
My favourite TV show starts at ____________.
I go to bed at ____________.

Hier trägst du „deine" Uhrzeiten ein.

2 Find the right clock and colour the boxes/the frames in the same colour.

- twenty past seven
- quarter to one
- half past nine
- eleven o'clock
- quarter past ten
- midnight

1 At home:

Can you guess the word?

Where is Sherlock? He is ...

- [x] sitting on the couch.
- [ ] in the bathtub.

What colour are the chairs in the dining room?

- [ ] They are blue.
- [x] They are red.

What animal is hiding in the wardrobe?

- [x] A bat.
- [ ] A snake.

What colour is the chair in front of the computer?

- [x] It is green.
- [ ] It is pink.

Where is the British Guard? He is ...

- [ ] lying in bed.
- [x] on the toilet.

2 At school:

How many can you see?

I can see three shelves.

I can see five pot plants.

I can see ten desks and nineteen chairs.

I can see two blackboards.

I can see one computer.

I can see two washbasins.

1 Recipe (*Rezept*): Cooffins (Cookies/Muffins) Soft cookies

Ingredients (*Zutaten*):

- 150g brown sugar (*brauner Zucker*)
- 1 egg (*Ei*)
- 75g unsweetened apple sauce (*ungesüßtes Apfelmus*)
- 150g flour (*Mehl*)
- 1TL salt (*Salz*)
- 100g oatmeal (*Haferflocken*)
- 1Pk. vanilla sugar (*Vanillezucker*)
- 125g soft butter (*weiche Butter*)
- 1 banana OR 1 apple (*Banane ODER Apfel*)
- ½TL baking powder (*Backpulver*)
- 150g white OR brown chocolate chips (*weiße ODER braune Schokotropfen*)

Step 1:

Put the sugar, the vanilla sugar, the egg and the butter in a bowl and stir until the mixture is creamy. Then add the apple sauce and keep stirring. (*Gib den Zucker, den Vanillezucker, das Ei und die Butter in eine Schüssel und rühre so lange, bis eine cremige Masse entsteht. Rühre dann das Apfelmus unter.*)

Step 2:

Peel and crush the banana/the apple with a fork and put it in the dough. Then mix the flour, the baking powder and the salt and add it to the mixture. Last, add the chocolate chips and oatmeal.
(*Schäle die Banane/den Apfel, zerdrücke sie/ihn mit einer Gabel und füge das Obst dem Teig zu. Vermische das Mehl, das Backpulver und das Salz und hebe die Mixtur langsam (löffelweise) unter. Füge am Schluss die Schokotropfen und die Haferflocken hinzu.*)

Step 3:

Place the dough with a spoon on a baking tray (+ baking paper). Make sure you leave enough space between the cooffins. Bake in a preheated oven (electric oven: 175 °C) for about 12 minutes.
(*Platziere nun den Teig mit Hilfe eines Löffels auf einem Backblech, das vorher mit Backpapier ausgelegt wurde. Achte darauf, dass genügend Abstand zwischen den Cooffins ist, da sie beim Backvorgang noch auseinandergehen. Heize den Ofen vor (E-Herd 175 °C) und backe die Cooffins 12 Minuten lang.*)

ENJOY!

2 Song: 5 little fruits jumping on the bed

Colour the picture! Egal wie du es anmalst, du kanst nichts falsch machen!

Key: 804

3 Song: Feelings

Find the match and use the same colour!

Key: 825

angry	take a nap
happy	say: "Oh no!"
scared	clap your hands
sleepy	stamp your feet

1 What's the weather like?

Colour the correct box!

sunny / rainy / windy	windy / cloudy / rainy
snowy / cloudy / sunny	foggy / sunny / cold
warm / cold / foggy	windy / snowy / cloudy

2 Do the crossword below!

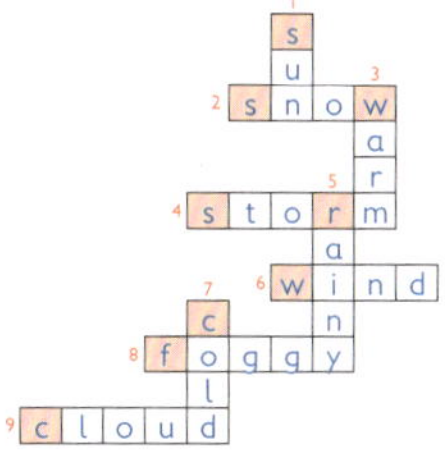

Across:	Down
2. Schnee	**1.** Sonne
4. Sturm	**3.** warm
6. Wind	**5.** regnerisch
8. nebelig	**7.** kalt
9. Wolke	

3 Find the weather-words and circle them!

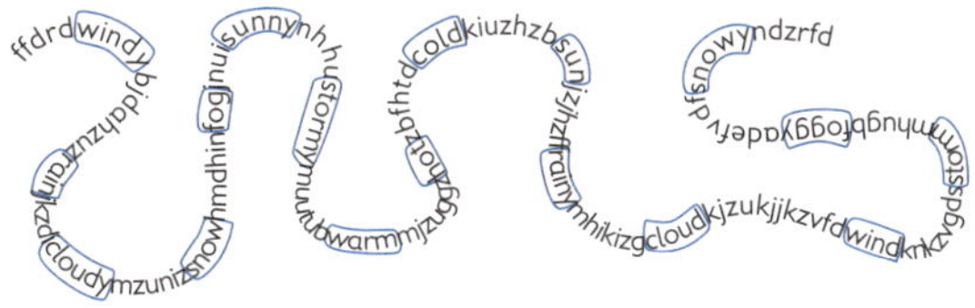

4 How is the weather!

The weather is *rainy*.

The *weather is sunny*.

The *weather is snowy*.

The weather is windy.

The weather is foggy.

1 Colour the word box. Use the correct pencil.

next to
between
behind
opposite
in front of

2 Where is the guard?

The guard is *behind* the tree.

The guard is sitting *opposite* his mother.

The guard is standing *in front of* the Palace.

The guard is standing *next to* the Queen.

The guard is sleeping *between* his teddies.

3 Read the sentences and fill in!

The school is *next to* the church.

The cinema is *opposite* the church.

The mall is *between* the cinema and the police station.

The kindergarten is *opposite* the school.

The playground (= Spielplatz) is *behind* the kindergarten.

1 Where is Sherlock?

Remember:
next to on top of
in front of in behind
between above
under

Complete the sentences.

Sherlock is hiding *behind* a tree.
Sherlock is standing *next to* the Guard.
Sherlock is sitting *in front of* the TV.
Sherlock is hiding *under* the bed.
Sherlock is standing *on top of* a mountain.
Sherlock is hiding *in* a box.
Sherlock is hiding *between* two bushes.
Sherlock is hanging *above* a thief (Dieb).

2 Now it's your turn. Read the sentences and draw!

The cat is sitting on the couch.

The cat is standing next to the dog.

The cat is sleeping under the bed.

The cat is sitting behind the tree.

The cat is in the fishbowl – looking for fish.

The cat is sitting on top of Sherlock's head.

1 Let's play!

Take the bus. Roll the dice again. *(Noch einmal würfeln)*

You spend all your money at Harrods. Go back to Start!

Visit the Buckingham Palace and meet the Queen. Skip ahead 7 spaces. *(7 Felder vor)*

You visit the London Eye. Because you're having so much fun, you miss a turn.

You take a boat on the Thames and it takes you to Big Ben.

You want to walk across the Tower Bridge, but it is up. Miss 2 turns.

Scotland Yard catches you and you have to spend a night in the Tower of London. Miss a turn. *(1x aussetzen)*

2 Answer the questions.

What is Big Ben?
☐ a clock ☒ a bell ☐ a church

Where does the Queen live?
☐ in the Tower of London ☐ in the London Eye ☒ in Buckingham Palace

Who guards (= bewacht) **the Buckingham Palace?**
☒  ☐  ☐ 

On which side of the street do you drive your car in England?
☐ on the right side ☒ on the left side

What is the British currency?
☐ Euro € ☐ Dollar $ ☒ Pounds £

What's the name of the British Flag?
☒ Union Jack ☐ Proud Mary ☐ Great Peter

1 There is always a reason to celebrate!

Help Sherlock to find the hidden words!

up ↑ down ↓ straight → ← diagonal ↗ ↘ ↖ ↙

U	I	O	K	M	N	I	H	O	M	H	E	T	S	J	C	R	H	G	K
C	H	R	I	S	T	M	A	S	K	O	V	X	I	N	A	E	H	N	B
V	U	B	B	D	G	V	B	O	N	W	Z	L	A	D	R	H	L	I	I
L	W	J	W	C	G	I	R	C	J	T	E	H	Y	C	N	H	U	V	M
I	Z	Q	H	H	R	P	U	G	M	V	S	L	N	J	I	M	G	I	X
U	M	R	E	T	S	A	E	P	E	E	F	U	E	D	V	R	O	G	R
H	J	M	H	F	K	J	R	S	H	F	T	M	A	I	A	G	P	S	H
E	Z	D	X	A	H	Y	R	A	W	A	F	Q	I	Z	L	Q	B	K	F
D	A	C	E	Q	X	A	A	D	K	B	L	H	X	J	P	V	I	N	J
Y	A	O	M	I	E	M	Q	D	D	S	E	L	A	X	C	K	J	A	A
N	V	F	D	Y	K	A	P	O	S	P	B	O	O	M	V	W	E	H	W
B	C	V	W	B	N	Z	N	E	S	E	X	S	H	W	S	J	E	T	H
S	O	E	H	L	A	L	J	A	Y	X	N	N	D	F	E	O	L	X	O
B	N	T	U	M	P	K	K	L	S	H	E	I	B	I	J	E	Q	U	W
S	V	S	Z	C	V	O	D	P	R	E	T	O	T	R	Z	K	N	V	M
U	I	F	B	A	F	F	I	V	G	V	K	X	I	N	Z	B	C	Q	T
E	Q	G	F	X	K	L	J	M	N	Q	J	Y	E	E	E	W	M	P	W
W	N	R	F	N	W	E	M	L	X	V	L	D	L	I	V	L	T	O	O
R	V	Q	J	I	V	X	F	E	H	X	K	F	Q	P	G	F	A	H	V
W	N	E	P	K	G	X	T	J	Q	M	G	L	W	K	P	A	P	V	E

birthday
carnival
christmas
easter
halloween
new year's eve
thanksgiving
valentine's day

2 Try to answer the questions correctly.

When is Halloween?

- [ ] September 31st
- [ ] December 24th
- [x] October 31st

Who hides all the Easter eggs?

- [ ] Father Christmas
- [ ] a ghost
- [x] the Easter bunny

What do Americans eat for Thanksgiving?

- [ ] fish
- [x] turkey
- [ ] pizza

What do girls often get for Valentine's Day?

- [x] flowers
- [ ] a dog
- [ ] a couch

3 Read the sentences and colour the correct picture.

The brown Easter bunny is holding a pink Easter egg.
The clown has green hair, a blue nose and a red hat.
Sherlock is on top of a yellow and orange Christmas ball.
He is wearing a red Santa Hat.
You get eight colourful balloons for your birthday.
The black cat is standing in front of the orange Jack O' Lantern.

Hier kannst du dir die Farben aussuchen. Alles ist richtig!

4 Find the match and number the picture.

① Halloween
② Christmas
③ Valentine's Day
④ Mother's Day
⑤ Easter
⑥ Birthday
⑦ New Year's Eve
⑧ Carnival
⑨ Thanksgiving
⑩ Father's Day

1 Song: The weather song

Key: 966

Colour the picture:

100: white
300: yellow
400: grey
others: blue

What can you see?

① sun
② cloud
③ snowflake

2 Halloween:

Roll the dice and draw a Halloween monster! Start with a circle for the body.

draw a head
draw an arm
draw an eye
draw a nose
draw a leg
draw a mouth with teeth

Hier kommen bestimmt einige gruselige Monster raus!

3 Listen and tick the right answer.

Write a sentence!

Key: 635

swim ☐
go shopping ☐

Lucy

skate ☐
read books ☐

Tim

play football ☐
play tennis ☐

Matt

sing ☐
dance ☐

Emily

Lucy likes to ______________.

Tim likes to ______________.

____.

____.

I like ________________, but I don't like ________________.

1 Time, time, time

I have to go to bed at ______________.

I have breakfast at ______________.

School finishes at ______________.

I want to go for a walk at ______________.

quarter past seven | half past six | quarter to twelve | ten o'clock

I get up at ________ o'clock.

I have breakfast at ____________________.

I leave for school at ____________________.

My favourite TV show starts at ____________________.

I go to bed at ____________________.

2 Find the right clock and colour the boxes/the frames in the same colour.

twenty past seven
quarter to one
half past nine
eleven o'clock
quarter past ten
midnight

1 At home:

Can you guess the word?

Where is Sherlock? He is ...

- [ ] sitting on the couch.
- [ ] in the bathtub.

What colour are the chairs in the dining room?

- [ ] They are blue.
- [ ] They are red.

What animal is hiding in the wardrobe?

- [ ] A bat.
- [ ] A snake.

What colour is the chair in front of the computer?

- [ ] It is green.
- [ ] It is pink.

Where is the British Guard? He is ...

- [ ] lying in bed.
- [ ] on the toilet.

2 At school:

How many can you see?

I can see ________ shelves.

I can s___ ________ pot plants.

I _____ _____ ________ desks and ___________ chairs.

I _____ _____ ________ blackboards.

__ _____ _____ ________ computer.

__ _____ _____ ________ washbasins.

1 Recipe (*Rezept*): Cooffins (Cookies/Muffins) Soft cookies

Ingredients (*Zutaten*):

- 150g brown sugar (*brauner Zucker*)
- 1 egg (*Ei*)
- 75g unsweetened apple sauce (*ungesüßtes Apfelmus*)
- 150g flour (*Mehl*)
- 1TL salt (*Salz*)
- 100g oatmeal (*Haferflocken*)
- 1Pk. vanilla sugar (*Vanillezucker*)
- 125g soft butter (*weiche Butter*)
- 1 banana OR 1 apple (*Banane ODER Apfel*)
- ½TL baking powder (*Backpulver*)
- 150g white OR brown chocolate chips (*weiße ODER braune Schokotropfen*)

Step 1:

Put the sugar, the vanilla sugar, the egg and the butter in a bowl and stir until the mixture is creamy. Then add the apple sauce and keep stirring.
(Gib den Zucker, den Vanillezucker, das Ei und die Butter in eine Schüssel und rühre so lange, bis eine cremige Masse entsteht. Rühre dann das Apfelmus unter.)

Step 2:

Peel and crush the banana/the apple with a fork and put it in the dough. Then mix the flour, the baking powder and the salt and add it to the mixture. Last, add the chocolate chips and oatmeal.
(Schäle die Banane/den Apfel, zerdrücke sie/ihn mit einer Gabel und füge das Obst dem Teig zu. Vermische das Mehl, das Backpulver und das Salz und hebe die Mixtur langsam (löffelweise) unter. Füge am Schluss die Schokotropfen und die Haferflocken hinzu.)

Step 3:

Place the dough with a spoon on a baking tray (+ baking paper). Make sure you leave enough space between the cooffins. Bake in a preheated oven (electric oven: 175 °C) for about 12 minutes.
(Platziere nun den Teig mit Hilfe eines Löffels auf einem Backblech, das vorher mit Backpapier ausgelegt wurde. Achte darauf, dass genügend Abstand zwischen den Cooffins ist, da sie beim Backvorgang noch auseinandergehen. Heize den Ofen vor (E-Herd 175°C) und backe die Cooffins 12 Minuten lang.)

ENJOY!

2 Song: 5 little fruits jumping on the bed

Colour the picture!

Key: 804

3 Song: Feelings

Find the match and use the same colour!

Key: 825

angry	take a nap
happy	say: "Oh no!"
scared	clap your hands
sleepy	stamp your feet

1 What's the weather like?

Colour the correct box!

- sunny
- rainy
- windy

- windy
- cloudy
- rainy

- snowy
- cloudy
- sunny

- foggy
- sunny
- cold

- warm
- cold
- foggy

- windy
- snowy
- cloudy

2 Do the crossword below!

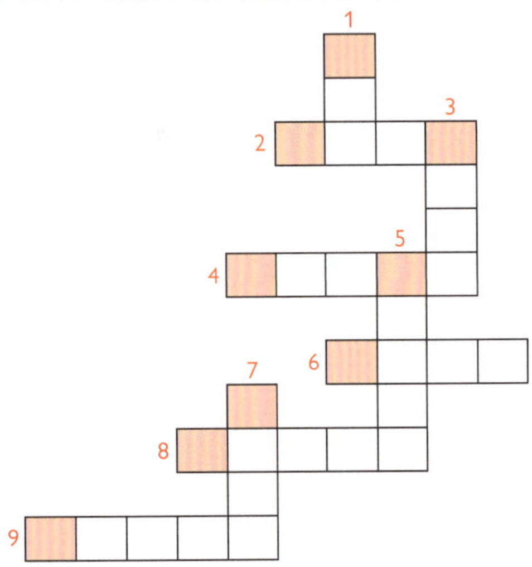

Across:
2. Schnee
4. Sturm
6. Wind
8. nebelig
9. Wolke

Down
1. Sonne
3. warm
5. regnerisch
7. kalt

3 Find the weather-words and circle them!

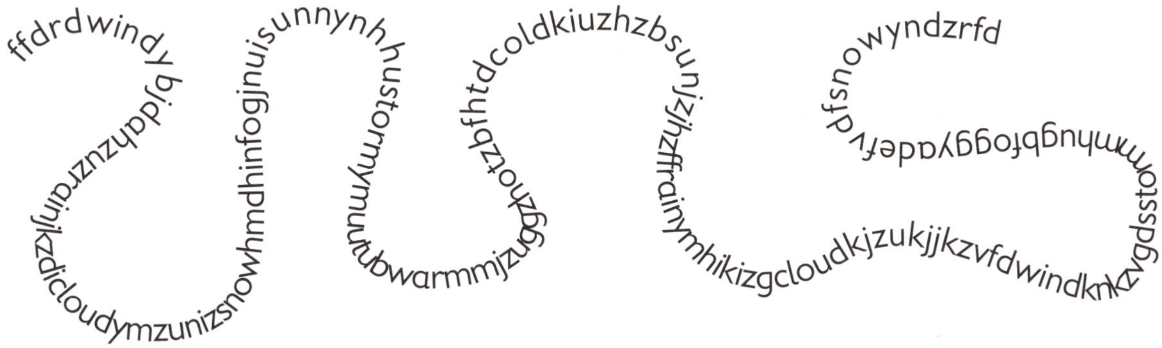

4 How is the weather!

The weather is ____________.

The ________________________.

The ________________________.

________________________.

________________________.

Where is ...?

1 Colour the word box. Use the correct pencil.

next to

between

behind

opposite

in front of

2 Where is the guard?

The guard is ________________ the tree.

The guard is sitting ________________ his mother.

The guard is standing ________________ the Palace.

The guard is standing ________________ the Queen.

The guard is sleeping ________________ his teddies.

3 Read the sentences and fill in!

The school is ____________ the church.

The cinema is ____________ the church.

The mall is ____________ the cinema and the police station.

The kindergarten is ____________ the school.

The playground (= Spielplatz) is ____________ the kindergarten.

1 Where is Sherlock?

Remember:

next to on top of

in front of in behind

between above

under

Complete the sentences.

Sherlock is hiding ________________ a tree.

Sherlock is standing ________________ the Guard.

Sherlock is sitting ________________ the TV.

Sherlock is hiding ________________ the bed.

Sherlock is standing ________________ a mountain.

Sherlock is hiding ________________ a box.

Sherlock is hiding ________________ two bushes.

Sherlock is hanging ________________ a thief (Dieb).

2 Now it's your turn. Read the sentences and draw!

The cat is sitting on the couch.

The cat is standing next to the dog.

The cat is sleeping under the bed.

The cat is sitting behind the tree.

The cat is in the fishbowl –
looking for fish.

The cat is sitting on top of
Sherlock's head.

1 Let's play!

Take the bus. Roll the dice again. *(Noch einmal würfeln)*

You spend all your money at Harrods. Go back to Start!

Visit the Buckingham Palace and meet the Queen. Skip ahead 7 spaces. (*7 Felder vor*)

You visit the London Eye. Because you're having so much fun, you miss a turn.

You take a boat on the Thames and it takes you to Big Ben. 

You want to walk across the Tower Bridge, but it is up. Miss 2 turns.

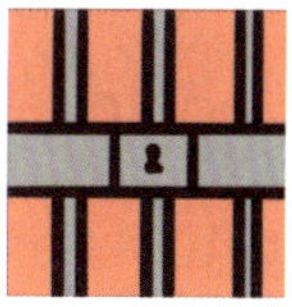
Scotland Yard catches you and you have to spend a night in the Tower of London. Miss a turn. *(1x aussetzen)*

2 Answer the questions.

What is Big Ben? 

☐ a clock ☐ a bell ☐ a church

Where does the Queen live? 

☐ in the Tower of London ☐ in the London Eye ☐ in Buckingham Palace

Who guards (= bewacht) **the Buckingham Palace?**

☐  ☐  ☐ 

On which side of the street do you drive your car in England? 

☐ on the right side ☐ on the left side

What is the British currency? 

☐ Euro € ☐ Dollar $ ☐ Pounds £

What's the name of the British Flag? 

☐ Union Jack ☐ Proud Mary ☐ Great Peter

1 There is always a reason to celebrate!

Help Sherlock to find the hidden words!

up ↑ down ↓ straight → ← diagonal ↗ ↘ ↖ ↙

U	I	O	K	M	N	I	H	O	M	H	E	T	S	J	C	R	H	G	K
C	H	R	I	S	T	M	A	S	K	O	V	X	I	N	A	E	H	N	B
V	U	B	B	D	G	V	B	O	N	W	Z	L	A	D	R	H	L	I	I
L	W	J	W	C	G	I	R	C	J	T	E	H	Y	C	N	H	U	V	M
I	Z	Q	H	H	R	P	U	G	M	V	S	L	N	J	I	M	G	I	X
U	M	R	E	T	S	A	E	P	E	E	F	U	E	D	V	R	O	G	R
H	J	M	H	F	K	I	R	S	H	F	T	M	A	I	A	G	P	S	H
E	Z	D	X	A	H	Y	R	A	W	A	F	Q	I	Z	L	Q	B	K	F
D	A	C	E	Q	X	A	A	D	K	B	L	H	X	J	P	V	I	N	J
Y	A	O	M	I	E	M	Q	D	D	S	E	L	A	X	C	K	J	A	A
N	V	F	D	Y	K	A	P	O	S	P	B	O	O	M	V	W	E	H	W
B	C	V	W	B	N	Z	N	E	S	E	X	S	H	W	S	J	E	T	H
S	O	E	H	L	A	L	J	A	Y	X	N	N	D	F	E	O	L	X	O
B	N	T	U	M	P	K	K	L	S	H	E	I	B	I	J	E	Q	U	W
S	V	S	Z	C	V	O	D	P	R	E	T	O	T	R	Z	K	N	V	M
U	I	F	B	A	F	F	I	V	G	V	K	X	I	N	Z	B	C	Q	T
E	Q	G	F	X	K	L	J	M	N	Q	J	Y	E	E	E	W	M	P	W
W	N	R	F	N	W	E	M	L	X	V	L	D	L	I	V	L	T	O	O
R	V	Q	J	I	V	X	F	E	H	X	K	F	Q	P	G	F	A	H	V
W	N	E	P	K	G	X	T	J	Q	M	G	L	W	K	P	A	P	V	E

birthday
carnival
christmas
easter
halloween
new year's eve
thanksgiving
valentine's day

2 Try to answer the questions correctly.

When is Halloween?

☐ September 31st ☐ December 24th ☐ October 31st

Who hides all the Easter eggs?

☐ Father Christmas ☐ a ghost ☐ the Easter bunny

What do Americans eat for Thanksgiving?

☐ fish ☐ turkey ☐ pizza

What do girls often get for Valentine's Day?

☐ flowers ☐ a dog ☐ a couch

3 Read the sentences and colour the correct picture.

The brown Easter bunny is holding a pink Easter egg.
The clown has green hair, a blue nose and a red hat.
Sherlock is on top of a yellow and orange Christmas ball.
He is wearing a red Santa Hat.
You get eight colourful balloons for your birthday.
The black cat is standing in front of the orange Jack O' Lantern.

4 Find the match and number the picture.

① Halloween
② Christmas
③ Valentine's Day
④ Mother's Day
⑤ Easter
⑥ Birthday
⑦ New Year's Eve
⑧ Carnival
⑨ Thanksgiving
⑩ Father's Day

1 Song: The weather song

Colour the picture:

100: white
300: yellow
400: grey
others: blue

Key: 966

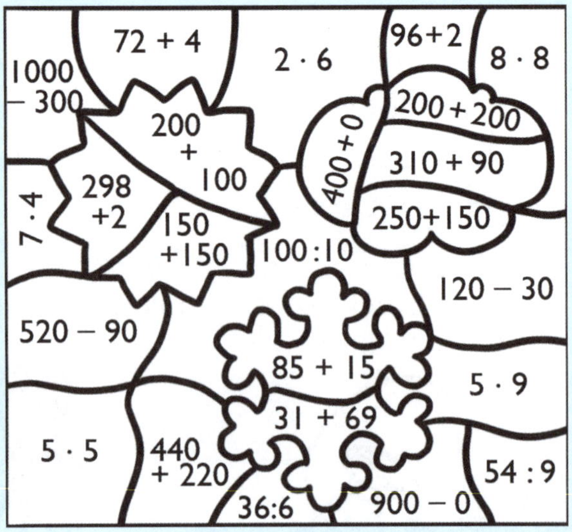

What can you see?

① ______________

② ______________

③ ______________

2 Halloween:

Roll the dice and draw a Halloween monster! Start with a circle for the body.

draw a head

draw an arm

draw an eye

draw a nose

draw a leg

draw a mouth with teeth